CATCH ME THE MOON, DADDY

LULLABY TO A NAUGHTY BABY

VENEZUELA

Lullaby, naughty child,
Your nonsense
Drives your mama wild.

Lullaby, arrurru,
What can Mama
Do with you?

Work all day,
Up all night,
By morning
Nothing's going right.

Lullaby, arrurru,
What can Mama
Do with you?

RIDDLES

P A R A G U A Y

Wonder, wonder,
What can it be?
Its tracks can't be seen
On sandy ground,
Although in straw
They can be found.

(the signs of a fire when a field is burned)

❧ ‹ › ❧

Wonder, wonder,
What can it be?
Thrown on a rock
It will not shatter,
But in water
It will tatter.

(paper)

THE RAIN HAS COME

ALGERIA

Oh, my brothers,
The rain has come.
Come, sit beneath the trees.
There are flowers;
I'll give you some.
Here is fruit...eat these.
Breathe deeply...
Hear the raindrops drum.
Play no more;
The rain has come.

HAIKU

J A P A N

In the ancient pond
I hear the sound of water.
A little frog jumps.

In the gentle night
Shrill chirrups of cicadas
Pierce even through rock.

8

CATCH ME THE MOON, DADDY

FORMER YUGOSLAVIA

Catch me the moon, Daddy,
Let it shine near me awhile.
Catch me the moon, Daddy,
I want to touch its smile.

— ◼ ◎ ◼ —

The moon must shine
From high above;
That's where it needs to stay —
Among the stars,
To guide them home
When they return from play.

— ◼ ◎ ◼ —

And as for you, my child,
With slender silver thread
The moon will weave
Sweet dreams, so you
May slumber in your bed.

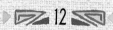

PONCHO

BOLIVIA

Poncho,
As Indian as my race,
Made with pure wool
Of the llama.
Bullfighter's cape
Of the strong wind,
You are my proud banner
Raised above the mountain.
I am your topmast,
Triumphant, alive.

SILVER KNIFE

CHINA

The Moon King's knife
Of silver bright
Floats over the waves
On a quiet night,
Floats to the fiery
Southern Sea
Where grows
The giant Pepper Tree.*
When the pepper seeds
To sea have gone,
The spring child sings
His first little song.

*The Pepper Tree is, according to Chinese fairy lore, the largest in the universe. In autumn, when the pepper seeds are ripe, the baby who was born in early spring is able to sing a little.

BLACK CROW

THAILAND

The Good Black Crow
Loves his friends, you know.
In his wandering he will find
Food, and call out to his kind,
Inviting them to share his riches...
Even a bite, but oh, it's delicious!

Look, my child, can you see
What this good crow
Shows you and me?
Love and share your things together
And happiness is yours forever.

AFSANA-SISANA

AFGHANISTAN

Afsana-Sisana
Forty birds yammer. . .
I cooked a very good stew
And ate it so nobody knew.
I gave some to a farmer to eat;
The farmer gave me some wheat.
I took the wheat to a mill;
The miller gave me flour, my fill.
With flour to a taghaar* I went;
The taghaar gave me some ferment.
The ferment I gave to a baker;
He gave me a loaf; the bread-maker.
To a shepherd I gave the bread;
He gave me a lamb instead.
The lamb to a wise man I took;
The wise man gave me a book.
The book I learned to read.
Now I have all that I need.

A taghaar is one who prepares yeast for bread.

MY BAMBOO
CANE COMPANION

KOREA

When I see my bamboo cane,
I feel fond welcome as again
In childhood, happy and serene,
I rode my pony-stick of green.
Now it stands beside the window so,
Or walks with me if I would go.

PUFIKI

NIGERIA

There is a little boy.
His name is Jon.
When you say, "Go to school,"
He refuses utterly.
Says he: "I will stay home
To cut fruit from the palm tree."
Pufiki! Pufiki! His name is Jon.
Pufiki! Pufiki! His name is Jon.

THIS LITTLE FINGER

COSTA RICA

This little finger
Found an egg,
This little finger cooked it,
This little finger sprinkled
Salt on it,
This little finger stirred it,
And this mischievous
Little one ate it!